Healing JOURNAL

The Journey to Restoration: A Walk Back into God's Anointing

Dr. Patricia E. Jones

First Edition

NEWMAN SPRINGS PUBLISHING
320 Broad Street
Red Bank, NJ 07701

First originally published by Newman Springs Publishing 2023

ISBN 978-1-68498-979-9 (Paperback)
ISBN 978-1-68498-980-5 (Digital)

Printed in the United States of America

This book belongs to

____

From

____

Date

____

Acknowledgment

I want to thank my pastor, Bishop Sherman Merritt Sr., for his dedication and love for the people of God helping me to better understand how to walk in a place with God.

I want to acknowledge my appreciation to my mother and sisters for their constant support and to my aunt Helen for opening a pathway of change for our family.

I want to thank my children—Sierra, Jasmine, Benjamin, and Cordrea—for their listening ears as I was seeking my way back to a place where God's power was restored in my life.

Last but not least, I want to thank my husband, SJ, for walking this journey with me these thirty years.

Introduction

I am writing this book because I realize that there is more that I long for in the Lord. I don't want to lose anything that the Lord has given me, but I want it to intensify. I feel that there are missing pieces that I need to recapture to help me on this journey called life. I have to reexamine my walk based on the choices I have made and the motivation for those choices. I understand that there is more that God wants to do in me and with me. When I stop moving with the flow of God's spirit, I can shortchange my life.

God came that I might have life and that I have it more abundantly. I asked the Lord, "How do I tap into the life that you have purposed for me to walk? Whom have you purposed me to be, and what are the gifts that have been placed in me that have not been utilized?" As I started this journey, God began to speak to me and I began to journal his words.

Day 1

Psalm 139:14 reads, "I will praise thee; for I am fearfully and wonderfully made: marvelous are thy works; and that my soul knows right well" (King James Version).

Today is a new beginning with Christ. As I choose to rejoice in this new day that the Lord has given me, I choose to refocus letting the shame, the fear, and the disappointments of my past go. I choose to walk in forgiveness. I chose to forgive those that have talked about me and tried to hinder my walk with Christ—those who tried to strip me of self-worth, those who led me into darkness, and those who caused me added grief to the point of suicide. I am thankful for God stepping into my life, leading me into the light, washing me, and filling the emptiness within me. God reminded me that I am fearfully and wonderfully made because I am made in the image of God. I am somebody. I am his child. He loves me, and he has made provisions for me that I can endure the tests and the trials of each day. These tests are just designed to make me better. I will become stronger because he is making me.

Day 1 Reflection

What do you need to let go?

Prayer: Lord, thank you for helping me to see the value that you have placed in my life and helping me to see that you are the one who made me and I belong to you. In the name of Jesus. *Amen.*

Day 2

First Timothy 2:8 reads, "I will therefore that men pray everywhere, lifting up holy hands, without wrath and doubting" (King James Version).

The road to spiritual restoration is not easy when we have been influenced by so many things. We first have to recognize the things that have changed our faith walk in another direction. The opposite direction of faith is fear. Where did the fear come from? Has it always been there, and does it linger when we stop covering ourselves in prayer? Prayer is the key to so many things. It is in prayer that we can access the presence of God. We cannot enter his presence in any way, except to be honest and open before him. Only then can we confess our shortcomings, weaknesses, and disobedience to him. We must seek his face and his grace to help us turn from our wicked ways. If we could do it on our own, he would not have had to die for the sins of this world. We were powerless and still are powerless without him. He is the Lord God that sees all: when we hurt, when we are abused and mistreated, or when we lie, steal, cheat, and compromise our stand. It is when we stop praying for his power that we fall short of what he has called us to be.

Day 2 Reflection

What is influencing your choices?

Prayer: Lord, thank you for helping me to understand the importance of daily prayer. You are my power source. I need your spirit to continue to lead, guide, and strengthen me. In the name of Jesus. *Amen.*

Day 3

Psalm 77:14 reads, "Thou art the God that doest wonders: thou hast declared thy strength among the people" (King James Version).

As I strive to find my way back to the place where I once stood with God, I have to remember his promises and his marvelous works and acknowledge him for who he is. You are the Lord of lords and should be placed in the highest position in my life. Lord, I acknowledge that you are the one with all power. You created the heavens and the earth. Only you know the direction I should go. You are a compassionate ruler. Lord, you are concerned with the fears of your people. Do I have the right to say no to your request? Do I give men more honor and respect than you, oh God? I acknowledge that there is no one or nothing greater than you. Nothing or no one compares to you. You are the righteous God. All your ways are right. You operate in truth, and only you have the answer to all my victories.

Day 3 Reflection

What or who is your life centered around?

____

____

____

____

____

____

____

____

____

____

____

____

Prayer: Lord, help me to yield to you as you guide me into the next victory. Teach me how to submit totally to your will and authority over my life. In the name of Jesus. *Amen.*

Day 4

Isaiah 14:24 reads, "The Lord of hosts hath sworn, saying, Surely as I have thought, so shall it come to pass; and as I have purposed, so shall it stand" (King James Version).

In order to move forward from the present state, I must let the things of my past go. I must let all misunderstandings go. I have to realize that everyone is not meant to be the same and that it is okay to disagree. Everyone is not created to perform the same purpose in this life. We all have different gifts and abilities that God wants us to use for his glory. Understanding this concept is needed to get me to a place where I can appreciate my purpose, and this will help me to walk into my destiny. I am an original. I am not supposed to be the same. I must remember God is sovereign. He does not have to give an account to anyone. He is free to do as he pleases. He made me for his glory, and his will is paramount to mine. I am the one who is dependent upon him for everything. He is my source and my strength, and without him, I cannot be victorious in this life nor fulfill his purpose.

Day 4 Reflection

What ways have you patterned yourself to be like others?

____

Prayer: Lord, you have placed something very unique within me. Your spirit has eternal glory and a light that cannot be put out. Let it shine with fulfilled purpose in my heart. In the name of Jesus. *Amen.*

Day 5

Psalm 51:6 reads, "Behold, thou desire truth in the inward parts: and in the hidden part thou shalt make me know wisdom" (King James Version).

Every day you extend your mercies to us with your loving-kindness. Daily, we are faced with new choices, and these choices determine the destiny of our soul. Adam and Eve had a daily choice to obey or disobey your instructions, just as Lucifer, the fallen angel who was adorned in beautiful garments and led your heavenly choir. As long as we continue to obey your instructions, blessings will continue to flow in our lives. It only takes one bad choice to change the direction of our life. We are so glad that when we make the wrong choices and rebel against your instruction, your grace provides mercy that keeps us from being separated from you forever. You did not stop loving us, but instead, you came to our rescue and delivered our souls. We were destined for hell when you heard our cry and delivered us from ourselves. We recognize we are no different from the prodigal son. He, too, understood he had fallen from the grace of God, so he humbled himself and repented of his actions. We must follow his example to restore the breach that we have created.

Day 5 Reflection

How have your choices separated you from God?

____

____

____

____

____

____

____

____

____

____

____

____

Prayer: Lord, I repent for my prideful and rebellious ways. Help me to live a life that is pleasing unto you. Wash me, cleanse me, and make me whole. I want to walk in obedience. In the name of Jesus. *Amen.*

Day 6

Psalm 1:1–2 reads, "Blessed is the man that walketh not in the counsel of the ungodly, nor stand in the way of sinners, nor sit in the seat of the scornful. But his delight is in the law of the LORD, and in his law doth he meditates day and night" (King James Version).

We must seek the counsel of God as we attempt to follow the leadings of the Holy Spirit. We should not choose the counsel of this world and sit in the seat of the scornful. We can delight in the law of the Lord if we earnestly seek his ways. He has signs along the way to guide us and let us know which way to go and which road to take. We must read the signs and carefully follow the instructions that are given to us. The road may be winding and hilly, and there may be some valleys we must go through. Regardless of how rough the road is, he wants us to stay on the course that he has placed us on. All other paths will lead to death and destruction. It is God's will that none of us perish, but each of us receives the gift of eternal life. We must travel to the end of our journey as we continue to search for the city that God has prepared for us. This city is a spiritual home for our soul where we will never die and live throughout eternity.

Day 6 Reflection

What signs has God shown you about your path?

Prayer: Lord, help me continue to walk in faith that I may show forth your glory everywhere I go. Lead me through the challenges of this life that I may obtain your eternal reward. In the name of Jesus. *Amen.*

Day 7

Second Timothy 1:7 reads, "For God hath not given us the spirit of fear; but of power, and of love, and of a sound mind" (King James Version).

On the road to restoration, we have to deal with the choices and mistakes of our past and how those things have influenced us to get to the place we are now. As we look around, we must be truthful with ourselves. Was it fear, was it pride, or was it both that influenced our decisions? We might say, "I don't have any fear." I know fear is not a spirit given by God because he has given us the spirit of love and of a sound mind. Fear is an enemy of faith. I am on a faith walk, so fear cannot be a part of my life. When we worry about what others think, about how we look, and about the unknown, these actions open the door to fear.

Fear opens the door for other spirits like pride. When we are so determined to do things our own way and no one can tell us anything, then we can open the door of pride. Focusing more on ourselves and what we lack is a recipe that opens the door to rejection. Fear, pride, and rejection are all direction changers. They move us from the lighted path of God's word. If we cry out unto the Lord, he promises he will hear our cry and deliver us. He knows how to place our feet back on the right path. God is showing us the way back to him. Cast your cares upon him for he cares for you. He will calm all the fears that are flooding your mind.

Day 7 Reflection

What doors do you need the Lord to close in your life?

Prayer: Lord, I cast my worries upon you. Calm my fears and give peace to my mind. In the name of Jesus. *Amen.*

Day 8

John 10:10 reads, "The thief cometh not, but for to steal, and to kill, and to destroy: I am come that they might have life and that they might have it more abundantly" (King James Version).

Jesus came that we might have life and have it more abundantly. When we think about our choices in life, we know that they lead us to eternal life or eternal death. What we say, do, and think determines the type of life we will have. The wrong choices can separate us from the love of God. This separation will lead us into a place of darkness—a cold, lonely, and empty place. While in this place of darkness, we cannot find any refuge for our heart's desire. We are therefore constantly searching, constantly empty, and constantly unfulfilled. The direction of our life can change when we choose to line up to God's Word and his instructions. His Word is like a lamp that brings clarity and understanding as it reveals the beauty and the warmth that can be felt in his presence. We have a sense of belonging and a joy that fills our hearts and soul. There is no emptiness but an overflow of peace within us. Love and kindness will guide the path we take, as our heart's desires are fulfilled. We are in a place of bliss that only God's presence can provide. This is the missing piece that we have been searching for in our lives. We desire to be restored to a place of completeness—made whole, mind, body, spirit, and soul.

Day 8 Reflection

What is your heart's desire?

____

Prayer: Lord, I know that you are the restorer of good things. Show me your will and fill me with your overflowing joy and peace. In the name of Jesus. *Amen.*

Day 9

Psalm 34:4 reads, "I sought the Lord, and he heard me, and delivered me from all my fears" (King James Version).

We seek to restore our relationship with Christ so that we may hear the sound of his voice. His voice soothes us and calms all our fears, reaffirming our faith and trust in him. He gently rocks us and wraps his loving arms of protection around us. Lord, you are concerned about your children. You know everything, and nothing gets by you. You know our ups and downs. Only you know how to keep us from falling. When we fall, you are always there to pick us up and mend our broken pieces. You comfort us with your words. We can hear your voice say, "It's going to be all right," just as a natural parent gives words of encouragement. It is followed by an embrace and a kiss for reassurance. God, your arms are wide open, ready to receive us today and to mend those bruises and broken areas of our lives. You remind us that it is going to be all right and that you are always nearby.

Day 9 Reflection

What pieces of your life do you need the Lord to mend?

____
____

Prayer: Lord, hear me when I cry. I need your help. Heal my broken heart and restore your strength within me. In the name of Jesus. *Amen.*

Day 10

Luke 1:37 reads, "For with God nothing shall be impossible" (King James Version).

We know that without obedience to God's Word, it is impossible to live a life that will please him. We realize we need him every minute and every hour of the day. But how do we reconnect with him when we have taken him for granted and allow ourselves to be separated from his presence. All disobedience that goes against the will of God is sin. Moving in the opposite direction of God's Word will cause us to drift apart from him. We long for his presence, the whisper of his gentle voice, and the daily fellowship that we once experienced as new believers. Our God never stops loving us, and His promises over our lives do not change. He is the same yesterday, today, and forevermore. The change that we seek is within us. We have to let go of pride and selfish ways. We must turn away from the desire to be in control and yield our mind, will, and emotion to him. Then we will see a directional change that takes us back to the presence of God. We will be in alignment with what he has for us, and we will be restored to the place of fellowship with him.

Day 10 Reflection

In what ways do you need to yield to God's spirit?

____

Prayer: Lord, I recognize that your presence is the most important thing in my life. Remove everything that separates me from your presence. In the name of Jesus. *Amen.*

Day 11

Psalm 118:24 reads, "This is the day which the Lord hath made; we will rejoice and be glad in it" (King James Version).

This is the day that the Lord has made. We should rejoice and be glad in it for many reasons. When we awakened this morning, we should have realized that God has spared us, although we have consistently rebelled and disobeyed his instructions. He has given us another day to correct our mistakes. As we reflect on yesterday, we recognize that it was God's hand of protection that was upon us. We don't deserve it, but he provides us with new mercies with the dawn of each new day. Let us not take his grace and mercy for granted. Let us stop and listen to what God is saying to us. Let's hearken to his voice and follow his lead. He says that if we are willing and obedient, we can eat the good of the land. It is the father's good pleasure to give unto us abundant blessings. Let us turn from our old worries and walk in truth and the light of his Word. He lights the pathway for us that leads back to him.

Day 11 Reflection

Where is God wanting more of his light to shine?

____
____
____
____
____
____
____
____
____
____
____
____

Prayer: Lord, I choose today to rejoice and be glad and to serve you with a grateful heart. Thank you for shining your light on me and directing my path. In the name of Jesus. *Amen.*

Day 12

Psalm 23:1 reads, "The Lord is my shepherd. I shall not want" (King James Version).

I am on a journey. I am in need of a Shepherd to guide me so that I do not wander or drift away. Guide me and keep me from being entangled in the thorns and the bristles along the way. Help me not fall off the cliff as I travel on rugged terrain. The Shepherd knows me by name. He knows my strengths and weaknesses, and he knows how to deliver me. He is the one who fights to set me free from the entanglements of life due to my disobedience. My disobedience causes me to wander away from my safe place and resist the directing of his staff. He still protects me from predators seeking to kill and destroy my life. He takes time to pull the burrows out of my coat and set me free. Although it is a painful process, he continues to show me his love and care, bringing me back to a place of safety. He is my Shepherd, and I shall not want.

Day 12 Reflection

What is influencing you to wander from God's safe place?

Prayer: The Lord is my Shepherd. I shall not want. He leads me beside the still waters, and he restores my soul. Thank you for your loving care. In the name of Jesus. *Amen.*

Day 13

Psalm 119:105 reads, "Thy word is a lamp unto my feet, and a light unto my path" (King James Version).

Have you ever been in the fog? You can be in a familiar area, but there is something about being in a place where you are not able to see clearly. You don't know what to expect, you are not sure where the next turn may be, and it's so easy to get off course and be led in the wrong direction. You may be traveling, not paying attention, and going past a crucial turn. We are in constant need of God's presence in our lives to guide us down every path and through every situation to ensure we continue on the right path at the right time so we do not end up on a detour. When we travel on a natural road and miss a turn, it takes a while to travel to a place we can turn around. When we travel on a spiritual road, we have lost hours, days, or even years. Sometimes it's not easy getting back on the right track because of the curves that exist on the wrong road. When the fog is lifted, we can see clearly where we are and we will still need God's help to find the path that leads back to him.

Day 13 Reflection

Where do you need God to provide clarity?

____

Prayer: Lord, light the way so we may see it clearly. Help us to listen closely to your instructions so we do not lose our way. In the name of Jesus. *Amen.*

Day 14

Joshua 18:3 reads, "And Joshua said unto the children of Israel, How long are ye slack to go to possess the land, which the LORD God of your fathers hath given you?" (King James Version).

As I reflect on the process that I have gone through in life, it has not been all glorious or flawless. There have been dark times and fiery trials that I have gone through to remove imperfections out of my life. I don't always understand the process, and I often get stuck in the same place instead of moving through it. I ask God, "How long must I go through this? Why are the same things continuing to happen in my life?" It is then that I need to be still and ask God, "What is it you want me to learn from this situation?" I must recognize that God is a good God and he doesn't want me to be unprepared for the next step of life. He will often hold me back to make sure I'm ready to take the next step. I must learn how to use the tools he has given me properly. Once I have mastered the required skills, I am ready to move forward and apply what I have learned for the next challenge. He wants me to be victorious.

Day 14 Reflection

What does God want you to learn from your past trials?

____
____
____
____
____
____
____
____
____
____
____
____

Prayer: Lord, give me strength as I go through my test and trials. Help me to understand and gain knowledge for the challenges that lie ahead. In the name of Jesus. *Amen.*

Day 15

Job 33:4 reads, "The spirit of God hath made me, and the breath of the Almighty hath given me life" (King James Version).

As I recognize who is the source and the strength of my life, it all leads back to you, oh God. You are the one who breathed the breath of life into me and I became a living soul. It is you who opened my eyes that I might see. It was you who opened my ears so that I might hear your voice. It was you who clothed me in my right mind that I might know the Creator of the universe. For it is in you that I live, move, and have my being. Apart from you, I am nothing, and without you, I will fail. As I look back at the failures in my life, I know it is because I have stopped out of your will. I have allowed a distance to come between you and I am no longer able to hear your voice. As I turn back to you and draw closer to your presence, I am able to hear your voice clearly. I am able to feel joy and gladness.

Day 15 Reflection

What has God done for you that makes you grateful?

Prayer: Thank you, Lord, for being the same yesterday and forever. Because you have not moved, I am able to return home. In the name of Jesus. *Amen.*

Day 16

Act 3:19 reads, "Repent ye therefore and be converted, that your sins may be blotted out when the times of refreshing shall come from the presence of the Lord" (King James Version).

I am beginning to feel the refreshing of the Holy Ghost. I am feeling the power of God returning into my life. The desire to pray and to read the Word is growing each day. He is satisfying the hunger and thirst of my soul. My soul is making a joyful melody. The heaviness of my heart is subsiding. I am beginning to see the breaking of a new day as I feel the gentle drops of rain beginning to fall on my face. It is the refreshing of the Holy Spirit. What a wonderful experience—the washing and the cleansing that comes with each drop. In the garden, the Lord sends the dew to fall upon it, to water it, and to give it what it needs to survive the day. God is giving me just what I need to be victorious today. I am being strengthened that I can withstand the test of the enemy. If I resist the enemy, he will flee from me. It is only through the power of the Holy Ghost that I am victorious.

Day 16 Reflection

What is God refreshing in your life?

____

____

____

____

____

____

____

____

____

____

____

____

Prayer: Lord, I repent of all my sins. Wash me and cleanse me from all unrighteousness and allow the refreshing of your presence to be restored in my life. In the name of Jesus. *Amen.*

Day 17

Second Corinthians 8:7 reads, "Therefore, as ye abound in everything, in faith, and utterance, and knowledge, and in all diligence, and in your love to us, see that ye abound in this grace also" (King James Version).

As I look over my life, I have to acknowledge that there have been many inconsistencies. There are days when I pray without ceasing, but there are also days filled with so many distractions that get in the way of my prayer life. I have to fight to make time for prayer. My body sometimes doesn't want to rise up early to pray. I yield my members and stay in bed to rest a little longer. When I do rise to pray, I seem to be at a loss for words. I'm so thankful that you know my heart. I can be honest and open before you. I desire to walk in truth. It is in those moments you reveal to me the things that I will need for the day and the cares that I need to cast upon you. You are still carrying me through every day, especially when I feel I don't have the strength to make it.

Day 17 Reflection

How has God been strengthening your life?

Prayer: Thank you, Lord, for being my daily bread and making provisions for me. When I am weak, you strengthen me and carry me forward. In the name of Jesus. *Amen.*

Day 18

Isaiah 26:3 reads, "Thou wilt keep him in perfect peace, whose mind is stayed on thee: because he trusts in thee" (King James Version).

It is another day's journey, and as I strive to remain focused, it is the Lord who is keeping my mind, will, and emotion intact. He has said he would keep me in perfect peace whose mind is stayed upon him. Let's start the day with the Word and let it cover me from head to toe. Let's bask in his glory. Knowing that today, nothing else matters, whatever happens, God is with me, guiding me and directing my steps. He is ensuring that today, I will have victory. Help me, oh Lord, to remain thankful and to serve you with a grateful heart—grateful for the restored fellowship and grateful for the removal of sins that separated me from his presence and the blood of Jesus that was shed on the cross for my sins. Thank you, Lord, for your Holy Spirit that has been sent to comfort and remind me of your Word and promises. The Word is designed to make me better, perfect, and establish me.

Day 18 Reflection

What is God wanting to perfect in you?

____
____
____
____
____
____
____
____
____
____
____
____

Prayer: Lord, I am truly grateful for your Word and the Holy Ghost that reminds me of your promises. I am not alone because you are with me. In the name of Jesus. *Amen.*

Day 19

Isaiah 58:12 reads, "And they that shall be of thee shall build the old waste places: thou shalt raise up the foundations of many generations; and thou shalt be called, The repairer of the breach, The restorer of paths to dwell in" (King James Version).

Life is cyclical. There are times when we must stop and remember all the challenges that we have faced and all the trials that the Lord has brought us through. At those moments in time, we thought we were not going to make it through. We have to say, thank you, Lord. God made a way every time we faced new challenges of strange and confusing days, even when we are on the brink of hopelessness. We look back to see God's grace and mercy. We know he has always been there and is still here giving us the strength to press straight ahead. All his promises are yea and amen. His Word concerning us has not changed. As we continue to align with his will, we seek to walk after the Spirit and we seek the kingdom of God. His Word says that all things will be added unto us and our souls will be satisfied with the pleasures that only come from God. He makes us know joy and gladness. He restores our souls.

Day 19 Reflection

What cycles keep occurring in your life?

____

____

____

____

____

____

____

____

____

____

____

____

Prayer: Lord, thank you for stopping the cycle that was leading me nowhere. You have given me direction and strength to help me move forward as your Spirit leads me. In the name of Jesus. *Amen.*

Day 20

First Samuel 16:7 reads, "But the LORD said unto Samuel, Look not on his countenance, or on the height of his stature; because I have refused him: for the LORD sees not as man sees; for man looks on the outward appearance, but the LORD looks on the heart" (King James Version).

When I come before the Lord, he searches the depths of my heart. I ask the Lord if he finds anything in me, take it out. What do I do when the Lord finds something in my heart? How will I respond? Will I deny my action like King Saul as he put the blame and responsibility for his actions on someone else? Saul said the people made him stand against the Lord. Am I willing to own up to my sins like King David? He confessed, "Lord, I have sinned against you. I have let you down and misused my power. I have let my desires overtake me and lead me down the path of destruction. The results of my choices have not only affected me, but it has also brought destruction to my family. I repent and ask you to cleanse me from my past sins and the desires of my heart. I ask you to blot out my transgressions, oh Lord. Please deliver me from my past and my wrongful desires. Create in me a clean heart, oh God, that I might serve you. You know my heart, oh Lord, and I want to be restored back to the right fellowship with you, my family, and my friends."

Day 20 Reflection

What things are you still holding on to?

Prayer: Lord, I come before you open and honest, confessing all my shortcomings and sins. I ask for your forgiveness. Cleanse me and restore a right spirit within me. Have your way in my life. I need you, oh Lord. In the name of Jesus. *Amen.*

Day 21

Psalm 51:12 reads, "Restore unto me the joy of thy salvation and uphold me with thy free spirit."

Today, another piece of the wall has come down. As I go through life, I know I will experience hurt, shame, and disappointment. I desired to never be in this place or experience anything like this again. So I ask for you to put up walls to protect me from these types of attacks. I did not realize that the same walls would make you distant and unreachable to me. I would lack the strength that comes with unity and a sense of closeness from a relationship with you. I limit my opportunities to experience the love and affection that is experienced in this relationship. I know I cannot isolate myself from emotions. I must face these feelings and ask God to restore the communication, restore the love, and restore the relationship we once had before humiliation, disappointment, or miscommunications stepped in. There are times when I find myself in uncomfortable situations. I did not know how to handle those problems. This is when I admitted I needed to go to God in prayer for the answers. He said when I cry unto him, he would hear me and deliver me from all my troubles.

Day 21 Reflection

What walls have separated you from the love of God?

____
____
____
____
____
____
____
____
____
____
____
____

Prayer: Thank you, God. You are a problem solver and a restorer of good things and relationships. Lord, please strengthen me, my communication skills, and the love within me for others. In the name of Jesus. *Amen.*

Day 22

Psalm 28:7 reads, "The Lord *is* my strength and my shield; My heart trusted in Him, and I am helped; Therefore, my heart greatly rejoices, and with my song, I will praise Him."

Every day, we must make a conscious decision to go forward. We must seek the Lord for strength, continuously. God promised he would provide our daily bread. He is the source that sustains us, our help in times of trouble. We all face challenges, but how we respond to those challenges determines our level of success. Do we cast all our cares on Jesus for he cares for us? Do we continue to stand on the truth of his Word and his promises? God said when you have done all that you know to do, keep standing in faith and keep trusting in his Word. Everything he has promised and every word he has spoken over us shall come to pass. His Word will accomplish what he has sent it out to do. Although weapons shall form against us, they will not triumph over us. The Lord is our Shepherd, our Protector against the wolves that arise to destroy us. We must continue to draw close to him and stay connected to the place where he has placed us. There is strength in unity and being connected to God.

Day 22 Reflection

How does God want you to respond to daily challenges?

Prayer: Lord, you have been my strength, and I cast all my cares upon you. You have never failed me. Help me to continue to trust you and move forward as you continue to restore me. In the name of Jesus. *Amen.*

Day 23

Ephesians 1:18 reads, "The eyes of your understanding being enlightened; that you may know what is the hope of His calling, what are the riches of the glory of His inheritance in the saints" (King James Version).

The eyes of my understanding are being enlightened. It is like awakening from a long dream in which the same part replays over and over so that I am without any control over the outcome. Today is a new day, I recognize. I wrestle not with flesh and blood but with spiritual wickedness in high places. I need God who is all-knowing, omniscient, and omnipotent to come into my life and take control. I need him to stop this vicious cycle and put my feet on the right path. His strength and protection are needed as I walk through all these trials and tribulations. I need him to fight for me evils seen and unseen. I know that the battle is not mine but the Lord's. He has the power needed to conquer anything and everything that comes against me today and always.

Day 23 Reflection

What answers has God given you to reflect upon?

Prayer: Lord, help me to rest in your Word and to abide under the shadow of your almighty wing. I want to grow and become all that you desire me to be. Lord, I thank you for opening my eyes so that I may see how much I need your guidance. In the name of Jesus. *Amen.*

Day 24

Psalm 46:1 reads, "God *is* our refuge and strength, a very present help in trouble" (King James Version).

On this journey, each day brings new challenges. We modify our next decision based on past experiences, mistakes, and the guidance of the Holy Spirit. We are learning each day how to trust the Lord more. We are learning how to believe him as we rest and walk in his Word. When storms arise in our life, it seems that he is not present, but God is always present. We must refocus and concentrate on the instructions that he has given us. His Word brings us through the storm. God's promises are yea and amen. He promised that he would never leave us nor forsake us, even when we can't feel him or sense his presence. We must be confident that he is there. We have to call unto him and believe he hears us. He will answer us and deliver us. God will take us through the fires that might be raging in our lives. God loves us, and he continues to demonstrate his love toward us. Listen for his voice, it will calm us.

Day 24 Reflection

What doors are opening for you that bring uncertainty?

Prayer: Lord, no matter what challenges the day brings, help me to remember you are my refuge and my strength. You know how to deliver me. I thank you for your provisions. In the name of Jesus. *Amen.*

Day 25

Second Chronicle 6:27 reads, "Then hear *in* heaven, and forgive the sin of Your servants, Your people Israel, that You may teach them the good way in which they should walk; and send rain on Your land which You have given to Your people as an inheritance" (King James Version).

I am still moving forward. Every day, God reveals more about me—the things that are hindering my growth and deliverance. I must face the fears of my past and forgive those who mistreat, ostracize, ridicule, or turn their backs on me. I must forgive those who have said I was nothing, treated me that way, and thought that I would never be anything. You have a plan and a purpose for my life. You did not allow me to be aborted as an unwanted pregnancy. God, you showed me how much you love me by lifting me out of despair. You let me know that I am fearfully and wonderfully made because I am made in your image. I have been created with a choice. Each day, I must be mindful of the choices I make. The choices I make affect not only me but also all those around me, especially the ones I love most. Help me to make choices that share the love you have given to me as a believer and follower of Christ.

Day 25 Reflection

What is stopping you from moving forward?

____

____

____

____

____

____

____

____

____

____

____

____

Prayer: Lord, you know the path that I take. Teach me your ways and your statues. Help me to forgive as you have forgiven me. Help me to be mindful of how I respond to you and others. Thank you for the grace and mercy that are needed for each day. In the name of Jesus. Amen.

Day 26

Matthew 6:33 reads, "But seek first the kingdom of God and His righteousness, and all these things shall be added to you" (King James Version).

Today is a closer walk with you than yesterday. I have to realize that my journey is not my own. My abilities cannot take me where you have destined me to walk. It is my complete surrender that will take me to the place of your anointing that I seek. You told me if I seek first the kingdom of God and all your righteousness, then these things would be added to me. Some may ask, "What are the things that can be added?" It is the desires of my heart and things my soul longs for. As you purify my heart and align it with your Word, my heart is being cleansed and focused. My desires are changing. I no longer desire the physical things of this world, but I am seeking for the spiritual things of God. I seek how to walk in the Spirit that I might please you, oh Lord. I pursue how to be a reflection of you in all that I do and say that you may get glory from my life.

Day 26 Reflection

What abilities does God want to expand in your life?

____

Prayer: Thank you, Lord, for changing my heart and transforming my mind. I realize you are in control of everything and you have designed me with a purpose. Let your purpose be fulfilled in my life. In the name of Jesus. *Amen.*

Day 27

Psalm 18:2 reads, "The Lord is my rock and my fortress and my deliverer; My God, my strength, in whom I will trust; My shield and the horn of my salvation, my stronghold" (King James Version).

I feel the changes that are taking place in my heart to renew a right spirit, yet I still sense a constant fight. I still fight against my old ways. I have to fight against those influences that make me want to quit. Those influences try to convince me it's not worth it. Those old thoughts say everything doesn't have to be centered around Jesus and the Word of God. Everything does need to be centered on God because he is the source of life—my strength, my rock, the guiding light that shows me the right path to take. Without him, I would still be struggling within myself with my fears and my doubts. I would be unstable, drifting in a hopeless spiral downward. I am so glad that God has held onto my hand. He has not let me go. He is still strengthening me through day-to-day challenges. He has proven to be faithful. What is placed into his hands he's able to keep it. It is because of him that I'm being transformed.

Day 27 Reflection

What does God want you to release to him?

Prayer: Thank you, Lord, for being my example of how to walk uprightly before you and your gift of the Holy Ghost that is able to keep me. In the name of Jesus. *Amen.*

Day 28

Luke 1:79 reads, "To give light to those who sit in darkness and the shadow of death, To guide our feet into the way of peace" (New King James Version).

On the road of life, there are signs that we need to pay attention to. These signs include our body, our minds, and our emotions. How are we responding to the situations and how do our situations affect us? We can say we are good, but are we really good? Everything is okay, but is it really okay? Our bodies can give us signs that indicate there is an imbalance going on inside of us. We may not be drinking enough water, we may not be eating the right foods, and we may be eating too many of the wrong foods that create toxins that are not supposed to be in our bodies. This opens the door for sickness, disease, inflammation, headaches, and pain to tell us we need to stop doing certain things. When our mind is constantly focused on the things that produce negative outcomes, it creates stress and indicates that we are flowing and moving in the opposite direction than God has intended for us. He has nothing but blessings planned for us. It is time to remove the things that are stopping the flow of blessings in our lives.

Day 28 Reflection

What could be added to balance in your spiritual walk?

Prayer: Lord, help me to be more aware of the signs that you give me. Help me to stop, refocus, and realign with your plan and your will for my life. You know what is best for me. In the name of Jesus. *Amen.*

Day 29

Psalm 51:10 reads, "Create in me a clean heart, O God, And renew a steadfast spirit within me" (New King James Version).

There come times in our lives when we must stop and deny ourselves our flesh access to the things it desires. We must fast from all those things that we crave. We have to make time to spend with God in prayer and reading his Word. Fasting is not an easy thing, but it allows us to concentrate on hearing God and seeking his direction for our life. Fasting allows us to say no to our fleshly desire and take back control over our will and our emotion. It allows our inner man to be strengthened. This is when we can truly allow God to show us where we have failed and guide us to the next steps. God will expose those secret sins that nobody else sees but him. As God uncovers those hidden sins in our lives, we have a choice to turn from those ways or continue. David chose to fall before God and cry, "Create in me a clean heart and renew a right spirit within me. Blot out my transgressions and make me know joy and gladness." We too must fall on our knees and cry to God to help us to let go any ways that are not pleasing in his sight and let him lead us into a new way of life.

Day 29 Reflection

How are your thoughts affecting your emotions?

____

Prayer: Lord, I offer a body as a sacrifice broken and humble before you. I repent of my sins, blot out my transgression, renew a right spirit within me, and restore the joy of my salvation. In the name of Jesus. Amen.

Day 30

Hebrew 12:1 reads, “Therefore we also, since we are surrounded by so great a cloud of witnesses, let us lay aside every weight, and the sin which so easily ensnares *us,* and let us run with endurance the race that is set before us, looking unto Jesus, the [a]author and [b]finisher of *our* faith, who for the joy that was set before Him endured the cross, despising the shame, and has sat down at the right hand of the throne of God” (New Kings James Version).

We are running a race with hope of obtaining the prize of the crown of eternal life. In the world’s race, there is only one winner. But with Christ, we all can be winners when we abide by the guidelines that have been set before us (the Bible). We must run this race with patience and determination. There will be hills that we have to climb, and there will be valleys we must go through. There will be dry places on the road as we run that to the end of the journey. We must stay focused so we don’t get distracted along the way by things that may cause us to want to stop. We must continue to press forward and know the Lord will continue to provide us with his supernatural strength to continue on. We can do all things through Christ who strengthens us. The race is not given to the swift but to those who endure to the end.

Day 30 Reflection

What is God asking you to persevere through?

____

Prayer: Lord, help me to keep heaven in my view. As I run this race with confidence that you will give me the strength, I need to make it to the end. In the name of Jesus. *Amen.*

Day 31

Ephesians 2:10 reads, "For we are His workmanship, created in Christ Jesus for good works, which God prepared beforehand that we should walk in them."

While we are moving toward the voice of God and seeking him for direction, we must also make sure we understand our purpose. We were created to do good works, which God has prepared in advance for us to do. As we align with his will and purpose for our lives, our natural abilities will begin to unfold. When the potential within us is released, it will cause a constant flow in our lives flowing like a river. The peace of God, the joy of God, and the love of God are necessary requirements to live and to walk with him in his presence. For in his presence is the fullness of joy and pleasures forevermore. This is the place that we have longed to be—a place where trusting him will lead us.

Day 31 Reflection

What purpose has God chosen you to walk out?

____

____

____

____

____

____

____

____

____

____

____

____

Prayer: Lord, lead and guide me today. Help me to put my trust in you without wavering. I know that you have everything I need: peace, joy, love, patience, and temperance. Thank you, Lord, for supplying all my needs. In the name of Jesus. *Amen.*

Day 32

Galatians 5:22–23 reads, "But the fruit of the Spirit is love, joy, peace, longsuffering, kindness, goodness, faithfulness, 23 [a]gentleness, self-control. Against such there is no law" (New King James Version).

Now that I understand my purpose in life, I have a new joy and a new passion for life. I desire to be the reflection of God. I desire to see as God sees me. I desire to do good and look for opportunities to share his love through words of encouragement and deeds. God is known by his charisma of love, joy, peace, kindness, goodness, and faithfulness. I want God's attributes to be seen in me. I must consciously decide each day if it will be filled with victories or defeat. When I use the tools that God has provided and the gifts he has placed in me, they always lead to victory. "There is now no condemnation to those who walk not after the flesh but the spirit" (Romans 8:1). If I allow my flesh to lead me, I open the door for defeat. My flesh lacks the knowledge that is needed to defeat the inner me and my enemy. I am dependent on God for every victory. Without God, I can do nothing, but I can do all things through Christ who strengthens me.

Day 32 Reflection

In what ways is God leading you to share his love?

____

Prayer: Lord, you have made me in your image. Let your Spirit have full reign in my life as I surrender my will. I know that your love, peace, joy, and self-control will be seen in me. In the name of Jesus. *Amen.*

Day 33

First Corinthians 3:10 reads, "According to the grace of God which was given to me, as a wise master builder I have laid the foundation, and another builds on it. But let each one take heed how he builds on it" (New King James Version).

Every great structure begins with a solid foundation. The foundation must be strong in order to withstand the pressures of external forces. The natural house and spiritual house have a parallel existence. Our spiritual house must also have a solid foundation, just like the physical house. Jesus must be the foundation that our life is built upon if we are to withstand the forces that come against us. Every foundation must be tested and tried. There will be times when problems will overflow our banks and result in a disastrous flood. The question then becomes, "Will our structure be able to withstand a breach in its foundation?" We also go through dry seasons in our life where the added pressures and extreme heat can be endured for long periods. Will we be able to withstand the heat of the fire and resist the temptation to give up? When the core of one's faith is being shaken, will one be able to continue to stand? God said he would build the church on a rock and the gates of hell shall not be able to stand against it. Let us accept your invitation to become a part of the kingdom of God. We are the church, and God's Spirit resides in us. His Word is the source and the strength of our foundation. We will survive the test if we remain confident and grounded in him. Keep looking unto Jesus, who is the Author and the Finisher of our faith. All the glory, honor, and eternal praise go to him.

Day 33 Reflection

How has God's presence allowed you to withstand the test?

____
____
____
____
____
____
____
____
____
____
____
____

Prayer: Lord, you are the master builder. You know exactly what I need. You have fortified me for the journey. Thank you, God, for giving me the faith I need to stand. In the name of Jesus. *Amen.*

Day 34

First Peter 2:13 reads, "Therefore submit yourselves to every [a]ordinance of man for the Lord's sake, whether to the king as supreme" (New King James Version).

I have come to the place of total surrender, not seeking my desires nor trying to reignite my passion. I release the reigns of my life unto you and yield to your perfect will. You are perfecting me for the purpose which you have created for me. "I am the workmanship created in Christ Jesus, to do good works, which he prepared in advance for me to do" (Ephesians 2:10). When you created mankind, you said mankind was very good. Based upon your Word, goodness was created and has always been a part of my character. Everything you purposed me to be is already within me. You are teaching me how to walk in the anointing that has been placed upon my life.

Day 34 Reflection

What things make you smile? What are you most passionate about?

Prayer: Thank you, Lord, for this opportunity to realign with your plan for my life. You desire for me to flourish. And my answer is yes, Lord—completely yes, with all my heart, my mind, my will, and my emotions. I want to align with your divine purpose for my life. In the name of Jesus. *Amen.*

Day 35

Joel 2:12–13 reads, "'Now, therefore,' says the LORD, 'turn to Me with all your heart, with fasting, with weeping, and with mourning. So rend your heart, and not your garments; Return to the LORD your God'" (New King James Version).

Lord, you have called me to fast to break the bounds of the wicked, to let the oppressed go free, and to undo heavy burdens. Lord, today, I renounce every covenant that I have made ignorantly with the enemy. I renounce covenants made by my forefathers that pledged allegiance to other gods. I renounced covenants made in secret-to-secret societies to obtain success or fleshly desires. Let the fire of heaven purify the altars of my heart and cleanse me from evil, perverse ways. Let the light of your Word shine brightly in my heart and in my soul. I erect an altar of praise to the Almighty God that lines up with your Word. I have chosen to serve you today and for all eternity. I recognize the blood of Jesus that was shed on Calvary to release my soul and to heal me from every infirmity of my mind and body. I have been made whole by the stripes you bore. The chains of the enemy have been broken by the blood of Jesus, and I am free to serve you, my God, my Savior.

Day 35 Reflection

What chains has God broken in your life?

Prayer: Lord, I present my body as a sacrifice. Burn up all the impurities within me. Let the fire fall that consumes those old ways that held me bound. I will offer you praise for what you have done in my life. In the name of Jesus. *Amen.*

Day 36

Romans 8:2 reads, "For the law of the Spirit of life in Christ Jesus has made me free from the law of sin and death."

Every day with Jesus is sweeter than the day before. God has released the limits I have placed upon myself. God has expanded my territory so that I may do more for him. God is helping me to seek him. I take responsibility for the choices made in my life—the good, the bad, the ugly, and the awful things that have brought me to this place of seeking his face. Now I am standing in the presence of God after repenting of my past mistakes, denouncing covenants with the gods of this world, and breaking strongholds over my life by the words I have spoken. I have been set free, and now my joy has been restored. For whom the Son has set free is free indeed. I am free to walk uprightly before him, and my ears are open to his instructions as I obey the guidance of the Holy Spirit.

Day 36 Reflection

What liberties has God released unto you?

Prayer: I thank God for the joy, peace, wisdom, and knowledge that comes with his Holy Spirit. Now I have the power needed to resist the devil. Your Word is a lamp unto my pathway and a light until my feet. You keep that which has been committed into your hands and present me faultless. In the name of Jesus. *Amen.*

Day 37

Hebrew 3:6 reads, "But Christ as a Son over His own house, whose house we are if we hold fast the confidence and the rejoicing of the hope [a] firm to the end."

Every day has its own challenges, but I am confident with the help of the Lord, I will be able to resist all the attacks of the enemy and remain focused on my purpose. My life has been placed into the hands of the Lord, and no one is able to pluck me out of his hands. I desire that your will be done in my life today and always. I do not want to take for granted your grace and your mercies you have extended to me today. Let me walk in obedience to your will. Help me to make better choices as I learn to walk and follow you. I know today will be a glorious day because you are in it with me. You promised never to leave me nor forsake me but to go with me into eternity.

Day 37 Reflection

How has the Lord restored your confidence?

Prayer: Thank you, Lord, for loving me and sending your Holy Spirit to lead and guide me into all truth as I walk out your plan for my life. In the name of Jesus. *Amen.*

Day 38

Psalm 7:6 reads, "Arise, O Lord, in Your anger; Lift Yourself up because of the rage of my enemies; Rise up [a]for me *to* the judgment You have commanded!"

It is a new day. A fresh anointing is flowing my way. I let go of my past sins and imperfections, and I am embracing my new way of living. I am not striving to fit the world's mold but conforming to the plan and the outline God has created for me. As he sculptures and molds me into the vessel he has created me to be, he has made me a vessel of value that will serve well in the kingdom of God. I have let go of my doubts, my insecurities, and my old ways of doing things. I'm walking in the newness of life and masking in his glory, for in his presence, there is fullness of joy and pleasures forevermore. I am striving every day to make it into eternity, to see my eternal reward for my endurance and diligently seeking him. There are promises that he gives to those who obey his commandments.

Day 38 Reflection

What promises are you expecting the Lord to manifest?

Prayer: Thank you, Lord, for helping me cast all my cares upon you, for I know you truly care for me. I believe that there is nothing impossible with God. In the name of Jesus. Amen.

Day 39

Psalm 145:5 reads, "I will meditate on the glorious splendor of Your majesty, And [b]on Your wondrous works."

I am aligning with your assignment so that the best of me reflects your goodness, your grace, your mercy, your patience, your loving-kindness, and your faithfulness. You have made me in your image. You have given me love power and a sound mind. My creativity comes from you. You are the master craftsman. I see all around me the splendor of your hand: the colors that are arrayed in the earth, the ocean and the seas, the beauty of the animals, the foliage of the forest, and the dew that rests upon the petals of every leaf. You know how to satisfy the needs of all your creation. You know exactly what we need and when we need it. The earth is the Lord's and the fullness thereof. You are awesome. God, your spoken Word is still being manifested before my eyes. It is performing all that you purpose, and it does not return to you void.

Day 39 Reflection

What things still need to be aligned in your life?

Prayer: The power of your spoken Word is still manifesting before our eyes today. You are the God of order, and I thank you for restoring order into our lives. In the name of Jesus. *Amen.*

Day 40

First Thessalonians 4:1 reads, "Finally then, brethren, we urge and exhort in the Lord Jesus that you should abound more and more, just as you received from us how you ought to walk and to please God."

I'm making a conscious decision to invite the Holy Spirit into my life to lead and to guide me today. I will actively listen to the instructions that are being given to me and to follow them with my whole heart. I choose to walk in faith and to stand up on the promises of God's Word. I choose to be an active participant in the good fight of faith. Faith comes by hearing and hearing the Word of God. I have put my armor on: the helmet of salvation and the breastplate of righteousness. My loins are girded about with truth, my feet are shed shod with the preparation of the Gospel of peace, and I have the sword of the Spirit to rightly divide the Word of truth. I will not fear what the enemy will do, for greater is he that is within me than he that is in the world. I can do all things through Christ, which strengthens me. There is no failure in God. I'm more than a conqueror. I am casting down every imagination and every high thing that would exalt itself against the Word of God. I have been anointed for the fight, and I am confident that I will win.

Day 40 Reflection

How will you maintain your relationship and continue to grow with Christ?

____

____

____

____

____

____

____

____

____

____

____

____

Prayer: Lord, you have brought this to this point, and I believe that this is just the beginning of greater. In the name of Jesus. *Amen.*

Conclusion

I am on a never-ending journey. My choices have to be intentional. I am continuously being made into who God has called me to be. God has not wasted any of my experiences. I have to trust him for every step of the way. I know that every day will present new challenges. The victory for each day will always be the same because Jesus is the one who gives me the strategies that I need for all situations. I have to remember that I can ask him anything. He promised me that he would hear me. When I call on him, he will deliver me out of every situation. I know that I have not arrived and the process of restoration is a daily process. I cannot take any day for granted. God has to continually be the center and source of everything in my life. I am still growing into who he has called me to be. As I continue to examine myself and yield to the leading and guiding of God's Holy Spirit, he will be glorified in my life. He has made all things beautiful in his time.

I challenge you to make each day of your life intentional, holding on to the basics that your faith has been built upon. First, establish a daily time to spend with the Lord in prayer, praying in your heavenly language asking him for wisdom, knowledge, and understanding. Also, include reading his Word daily so you can be established and equipped with the *word* of truth. We must not forget fasting, which helps you to deny your flesh and strive to stay aligned as you walk according to his will. It is a daily fight, but with God, you can do all things.

About the Author

Dr. Patricia E. Jones is a native Texan. She serves her community in many ways. She has been in public education for over twenty years as a teacher, coach, mentor, instructional leader, assistant principal, and professor. She is known in the community as Dr. Jones.

Her community service extends to teaching Sunday school and ministering in the prison and nursing homes. She sponsors a yearly book drive to collect books for the local children's hospital. Her desire to support those in need prompted a college care package to aid students during periods when food is not provided on campus.

She has served as a chairperson and member for two boards in Tennessee to support community partnerships and sponsored a charter high school.

Dr. Jones is looking forward to expanding her educational support as an author, consultant, curriculum designer, and administrator.

www.ingramcontent.com/pod-product-compliance
Lightning Source LLC
LaVergne TN
LVHW050937080826
845145LV00004B/1307

9781684989799